# Prayers for the Seasons

*Lois Kikkert, O.P.*

PILGRIMAGE

**PAULIST PRESS**

**New York/Ramsey**

ISBN: 0-8091-9306-X

Published by Paulist Press
545 Island Road
Ramsey, New Jersey 07446

Printed and bound in the United States of America

All Scripture references taken from *Saint Joseph Edition of
The New American Bible,* Catholic Book Publishing Co., New York, 1970

# Contents

# Introduction

Time has been accelerated to the point that months seem to end on the day after they begin; yet God's design for the seasons still unfolds at the pace he originally ordered.

One can note by observing the gentle flow of God's creation, that the seasonal changes are energized by what precedes them and are coaxed forward by what follows. The blossoms of life which appear in spring were buried beneath the visible death signs of winter. These spring buds permit the fullness of life to come from within, and summer exposes the total capacity of creation. The magnificent autumn foliage provides a delicate transition for the shedding of the old, announcing that after a time of rest, the blossoms of life will burst forth anew.

Though the beauty of nature visibly speaks the change of seasons, some geographic regions within a nation depend upon other signs to record the passing of time. Perhaps for many people it is an influx of vacationers or the exportation of local produce or the arrangement of the constellations in the night sky that marks the blending of the seasons.

Regardless of the manner in which nature reveals the changes, one is certain that the cyclic pattern is imbedded in our individual lives; God's creative invention of the seasons is mirrored in the journeys of human beings. Each person can witness to the springs and summers, the autumns and winters of life.

On still a larger scale, the Author of life breathes his seasonal design into the parish community. God calls his people to enable each other to *be* the events of summer, fall, and winter in order to *become* the blossoms of life for the parish.

It is hoped that this little book of prayers will provide some help as you journey within to touch God's presence and as you journey forward to touch his presence in each other.

The PILGRIMAGE series is edited by the Small Christian Community Department of the Office of Pastoral Renewal of the Archdiocese of Newark. The pastoral vision of the archdiocese highlights small Christian communities as an integral part of ongoing parish life and encourages the parish to be a community made up of many small communities.

# Suggestions for Leader

The God who dwells within us constantly calls us to a deeper relationship with him. As he transforms us into his image he moves us to share his life with all whom we meet. Implied in the Lord's call is a need for prayer, both personal and communal. It is hoped that the following suggestions will provide help in using this book.

## Preparation for a Meeting

Prior to the meeting time the leader previews the prayer session. S/he could opt to line-up the record/cassette and the needed equipment or transfer this responsibility to another member of the group.

## Day of Meeting

Allowing sufficient time before the arrival of the group, the leader or another member arranges the meeting room for prayer.

## Call to Prayer

Though each session provides a suggestion for the call to prayer, the leader can make adjustments to satisfy needs of the group.

## Scripture

A Bible should be available for each gathering. Perhaps the leader could enthrone the Bible on a simple stand and place a lighted candle near the Bible. For variations the candle could be the color appropriate to the liturgical season and a plant or simple floral piece could be placed on the stand.

The person who proclaims the Word should have time to prepare the reading.

## Reflection

Each session provides instructions for reading the reflection; however, the leader can choose an alternate process to satisfy the needs of the group.

## Sharing

The leader invites the members of the community to silently read all the questions, providing sufficient time for personal reflection. The leader will sense the amount of time appropriate for the group and will call the members to a sharing of responses. The leader allows individuals to choose the question with which they feel comfortable. Not all the given questions need to be addressed.

## Petitions

The leader could invite spontaneous petitions of praise, thanksgiving, or intercession.

## Prayer

The leader invites the community members to pray the closing prayer in unison. At times it might be appropriate to have an individual pray this prayer.

## Suggested Song

The songs which have been suggested are Scripture-based and provide another means by which God speaks. The leader encourages the people to allow the words of the song to enter their hearts, thus enriching the prayer experience which they are sharing.

The leader would borrow the record/cassette from the parish resource center.

# A Sign of Fidelity...
## A Presence That Remains

### Call to Prayer:
(The leader calls the people to prayer by providing a quiet, gentle atmosphere for a few moments.)

### Suggested Song:
*Yahweh, the Faithful One*

**Refrain**
Yahweh's love will last forever,
His faithfulness till the end of time.
Yahweh is a loving God.
Yahweh, the faithful one.

1. Have no fear, for I am with you;
   I will be your shield.
   Go now and leave your homeland,
   For I will give you a home.

2. You shall be My chosen people,
   And I will be your God.
   I will bless your name forever
   And keep you from all harm.

3. Look up and see the heavens
   And count the stars if you can.
   Your name will be even greater,
   Greater than all these stars.

4. See now the land before you,
   Rich.with food and rain.
   No longer must you wander,
   For this will be your home.

Record Album/Cassette *Neither Silver Nor Gold*ᶜ 1970 Daniel L. Schutte, S.J., North American Liturgy Resources, Phoenix, Arizona 85029

### Opening Prayer:
(The leader prays spontaneously or uses the following prayer.)

God, our Father, we revere your presence within us and among us. We praise and thank you for this moment in time — a moment which you have seen from the beginning, yet a moment which is only becoming known to us. We are awed by the knowledge that you, our God, choose to dwell within each of us.

Stir up within us the power of your Spirit so that we will open ourselves to accept the many ways in which you will now gift us.

## Scripture:

(Reading from the Bible, the leader reverently proclaims the single verse which is indicated below and provides a few moments of silence so the Word of God can be absorbed and savored.)

## Lamentations 3:22a, 23

"The favors of the Lord are renewed each morning, so great is his faithfulness."

## Reflection:

(The leader could opt to read this section aloud or invite another member of the community to participate. Whoever assumes the responsibility should have time prior to the gathering to prepare for the reading.)

When a young child awakens before daylight has removed the shades of night, s/he may be frightened. If the teddy bear or the favorite doll cannot be located, fear mounts. If the wind is whistling unfamiliar tunes through the opened window, fear reaches new heights. If stomach pains or a fever grips the little body, the child cries out for comfort. A parent, hearing the plea, responds immediately. Isn't this just what the child expected! Previous experiences of anxiety, times of discomfort, moments of fear, twinges of pain have always been absorbed by the parent's love. Loneliness has always been healed by the parent's quiet presence. Remembrance of these events forces the child to call out again; and true to expectation — Mommy or Daddy was there. The child never questions how the parent sensed the need; s/he is content with the response.

Oh, that we might trust in this simple fashion! That we might realize the faithful parent is an image of the faithfulness of our God! That we might delight in the knowledge that his favor rests on each of us and that he constantly pours out his love!

## Sharing:

(The leader invites the members of the community to silently read all the questions, providing sufficient time for personal reflection. The leader calls for a sharing of responses, allowing the members to choose the questions with which they feel comfortable. Not all the questions need to be addressed.)

- What are some of the signs of God's faithfulness to the movement of the universe which appear each day?
- How does the Lord renew you each morning?
- How has a friend been a source of building up your level of trust?
- Share an example of a time when someone's fidelity was a graced moment for you.
- How can we be instruments of God's faithfulness to the people of our parish community?

## Prayer:

(All) Lord God, our Father, we praise and thank you for your presence within us and among us. It is so comforting to feel your love and to see the signs of your faithfulness in our lives. You speak in such gentle ways; you touch us with your healing power; you dispel our fears by gifting us with courage to face our responsibilities. We acknowledge your special favor in creating us in your image and likeness. Lord, point out to us ways in which we can be your instruments of faithfulness to each other and to all whom we serve in this parish community. We ask this in the name of your Son, Jesus, who lives and works with you in the unity of the Holy Spirit, as our God. Amen.

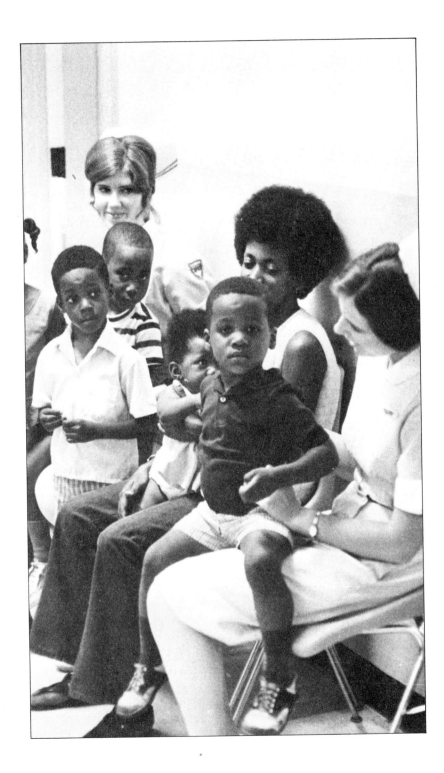

# An Awesome Image...
## A God Who Dances

**Call to Prayer:**
(The leader calls the people to prayer by providing a quiet, gentle atmosphere for a few moments.)

**Opening Prayer:**
(The leader prays spontaneously or uses the following prayer.)

God, our Father, we revere your presence within us and among us. We praise and thank you for this moment in time — a moment which you have seen from the beginning yet a moment which is only becoming known to us. We are awed by the knowledge that you, our God, choose to dwell within each of us.

Stir up within us the power of your Spirit so that we will open ourselves to accept the many ways in which you will now gift us.

**Scripture:**
(Reading from the Bible, the leader reverently proclaims the single verse which is indicated below and provides a few moments of silence so the Word of God can be absorbed and savored.)

**Zephaniah 3:17**
"He will rejoice over you with gladness, and renew you in his love. He will sing joyfully because of you..."

**Reflection:**
(The leader could opt to read this section aloud or invite another member of the community to participate. Whoever assumes the responsibility should have time prior to the gathering to prepare for the reading.)

A son who has drifted into the world of drugs, an unwed daughter who reveals her pregnancy, a child who is imprisoned for a robbery would find it difficult to believe that his/her parents would sing joyfully because of their offspring.

A sinner doubts that his/her God would find favor with the prodigal child. Yet, God tells us through the prophet Zephaniah that he rejoices over each of us with gladness. He sings joyfully because of us, and is moved to renew us in his love.

8

## Suggested Song:
*And the Father Will Dance*
Rev. Carey Landry

> **Refrain**
> And the Father will dance
> As on a day of joy.
> He will exult over you
> And renew you by his love.

1. Shout for joy, all you, his people
   Sing aloud and exult with all your heart
   For Yahweh, your God is in your midst. (Refrain)

2. You have no more evil to fear.
   You have no more evil to fear.
   Do not let your hands fall limp,
   for Yahweh, your God is in your midst. (Refrain)

3. And when the time comes I will rescue the lame,
   And when the time comes I will gather the strays,
   And when the time comes I will be your guide.
   I will gather you in and give you renown among
   All peoples. (Refrain)

Record Album/Cassette *Abba, Father* © 1977 North American Liturgy Resources, 2110 W. Peoria Avenue, Phoenix, AZ 85029

## Sharing:
(The leader invites the members of the community to silently read all the questions, providing sufficient time for personal reflection. The leader calls for a sharing of responses, allowing the members to choose the questions with which they feel comfortable. Not all the questions need to be addressed.)

• What does this Scripture passage mean for you at this time?
• How might God be opening you to receive his love?
• How might God be opening you to be his instrument to renew the lives of others? *(e.g., staff, parish council, committees, parish, family member)*

## Prayer:
(All) Lord God, in this moment we stand in awe at the knowledge of your presence. At times when we are downcast, discouraged, or even at odds with one another — failing to image you — you are in our midst. You can never not be here! How incredible is this knowledge! Your power stands waiting to be released so as to renew us in your love.

# The Bonus Prize...
## A God Who Gifts with Holiness and Wholeness

### Call to Prayer:

(In one section of the meeting room, arrange a sufficient number of chairs in a circle and have instrumental music playing softly. This setting will help to create a prayerful atmosphere into which the leader calls the people.)

### Opening Prayer:

God, our Father, you are all-gentle, we praise you.
you are all-holy, we thank you.
you are all-loving, we glorify you.
you are all-giving, we open ourselves to you.

### Suggested Song:

*You Are Near*
Dan Schutte, S.J.

#### Refrain:
Yahweh, I know You are near,
Standing always at my side.
You guard me from the foe,
And You lead me in ways everlasting.

Lord, You have searched my heart,
And You know when I sit and when I stand.
Your hand is upon me protecting me from death,
Keeping me from harm. (Refrain)

Where can I run from Your love?
If I climb to the heavens You are there;
If I fly to the sunrise or sail beyond the sea,
Still I'd find You there. (Refrain)

You know my heart and its ways,
You who formed me before I was born
In the secret of darkness before I saw the sun
In my mother's womb. (Refrain)

Marvelous to me are Your works;
How profound are Your thoughts, my Lord.
Even if I could count them, they number as the stars,
You would still be there. (Refrain)

Record Album/Cassette *Neither Silver Nor Gold* © 1971 North American
Liturgy Resources, Phoenix, AZ 85029

## Scripture:

(The leader or a volunteer approached earlier proclaims the
Scripture passage from the Bible.)

## 2 Timothy 1:9

"God has saved us and has called us to a holy life, not
because of any merit of ours but according to his own
design — the grace held out to us in Christ Jesus before the
world began."

## Reflection:

(The leader invites the people to read the reflection silently
at a slow, meditative pace, suggesting that they move on to
personally reflect on the questions.)

Often we get caught up in the prize-mentality of our age.
Cereal boxes, bottle caps, candy wrappers, and other gimmicks
entice us to try for the big wins; we purchase the product
which announces a bonus within. We work side-by-side with
people who ask, "What's in it for me?" Social rules suggest
trade-offs, measured accurately so as to exclude generosity.
Our productivity insures just payments; we earn our
recompense. At times we are so embedded in the conveyor belt
mentality that we deal with other humans as if they were
manufactured items. We portion out rewards on a report card
basis, careful to adjust the plus or minus as one has
merited it.

In a given moment we are willing to hear the words which
Paul wrote to Timothy, "God called us according to his own
design." There are no actions we perform, no words we utter,
no efforts we make that merit God's gifts; he pours them out
freely; we need only to accept them. This concept may be
difficult to grasp because of the reward/punishment system
which is part of our background. A lack of comprehension
does not eradicate the truth — "God has saved us and has
called us to a holy life" — not because we desire holiness, not
because we have merited holiness — but because he loves us!
Our affirmative response to his call compels us to live a life
which is whole and holy.

## Sharing:

(Having provided sufficient time for a meditative reading of the reflection and silent response to the questions, the leader calls for verbal input, always allowing participants to choose the question with which they feel comfortable.)

- What do you think are some characteristics of a life of holiness?
- What positive actions must you take in order to live a whole and holy life?
- How do you see your present position (as member of staff, parish council, society, committee) as fitting into God's design?
- What can we (as staff, council, society, committee) do to respond to God's call to serve his people?

## Litany of Thanksgiving:

For having called us, we thank you, Father.
For the gift of your Son, we thank you, Father.
For dwelling within us, we thank you, Father.
For using us to serve others, we thank you, Father.
For your power at work among us, we thank you, Father.
(Individuals add phrases)

## Prayer:

(All) Lord God, it is awesome to hear the message that you have chosen each of us, not because we merited the call, but because you have designed your plan to include us. Give us courage to release the shackles which bind us to working for praise. Keep us, Lord, from judging the performance levels of others. Open us to receive your power to serve this community without counting the cost, always mindful that all we do and say is for your honor and glory and the building of your kingdom here on earth. We make our prayer through Jesus Christ. Amen.

# Community Persons...
## Ones Who Knead Each Other

## Call to Prayer:

(The leader calls the people to focus on God's presence within and among them, and provides a few minutes of quieting time.)

(The leader encourages the people to allow the words of the song to enter their hearts.)

## Suggested Song:

*Abba! Father!*
Rev. Carey Landry

**Refrain**
Abba, Abba, Father.
You are the potter;
We are the clay,
The work of Your hands.

Mold us, mold us and fashion us
Into the image of Jesus Your Son,
Of Jesus Your Son. (Refrain)

Father, may we be one in You.
May we be one in You
As He is in You
And You are in Him. (Refrain)

Glory, glory and praise to You
Glory and praise to You
Forever, amen,
Forever, amen. (Refrain)

Record Album/Cassette *Abba! Father!*© 1977 North American Liturgy Resources, 2110 W. Peoria Avenue, Phoenix, AZ 85029

## Opening Prayer:

(The leader prays the following prayer.)

Lord God, keep our vision clear. Help us to recall in this moment that you are the potter and we are the clay. You are molding each of us in your image. You are always a patient and gentle God who loves us as we are — not as we should be.

Remind us of this as we interact during this meeting (substitute the nature of the gathering). Make us pliable so we will be open to hear each other's opinions, always keeping in mind that you are present within each of us. We pray in the Name of your Son Jesus. Amen.

## Scripture:

(Reading from the Bible, the leader reverently proclaims the single verse which is indicated below and provides a few moments of silence so the Word of God can be absorbed and savored.)

### Jeremiah 18:4-6b

"...he tried again, making of the clay another object of whatever sort he pleased...like clay in the hand of the potter, so are you in my hand."

## Reflection:

(The leader invites the members of the community to read the reflection silently at a slow, meditative pace, suggesting that they move on to personally reflect on the given questions.)

One who works in a garden knows the texture of the soil; one who makes bread feels the proper consistency of the dough; one who dabbles in oil painting moves the colors on the canvas to achieve the desired effect. Anyone who uses the gift of creativity is aware of the process of building and undoing, of starting again and at times casting aside the work in order to move in a new direction. A writer scratches out words, inserts new ones, steps apart from the creative piece, and returns with new insight. A film producer splices together certain frames which will be pleasing to the audience. To be an author of any work requires effort, patient endurance, tolerance of self and others, and the willingness to receive constructive criticism.

We are authors — we are designers — we are giving shape to this *(proposal, goal-setting, parish mission statement, ministry, parish function)*. We will use time and energy to coax the process forward. We will shape and smooth out the rough spots. Perhaps part of the process will demand our scrapping the present plans, starting anew, and being patient with each other — remembering that each of us brings forth his/her special gifts to be used in completing this assignment.

15

## Sharing:

(Having provided sufficient time for a meditative reading of the reflection and questions, the leader allows the people to respond to selected questions.)

- What more do we need to know about our parishioners as we begin to design this *proposal, mission statement, parish function, ministry, or participate in this meeting?*
- What special gift am I to this group for this particular assignment?
- What alternate plans can I suggest which will help in completing this work?

## Litany of Praise:

(The leader invites the people to pray the litany together, adding spontaneous phrases.)

For your faithfulness to us, we praise you, Lord.
For your gift of creativity, we praise you, Lord.
For molding us in your image, we praise you, Lord.
For_____, we praise you, Lord.
We pray in the Name of your Son, Jesus.

# The Core of Commitment...
## A Heart That Loves

### Call to Prayer:

(The leader prepares for this time of prayer by calling the members into a quiet, restful atmosphere. S/he gently reminds the people to place all distractions before the Lord.)

### Opening Prayer:

Lord God, we praise and thank you for these moments of quiet during which you will reveal yourself to us in new ways. Strengthen us so we will open our hearts to receive you through your Word and through each other.

### Scripture:

(Reading from the Bible, the leader reverently proclaims the passage. S/he provides a few moments of silence, then invites the members of the group to silently read the reflection and questions.)

### Jeremiah 31:33b-34

"I will place my law within them, and write it upon their hearts; I will be their God and they shall be my people. No longer will they have need to teach their friends and kinsfolk how to know the Lord. All, from least to greatest shall know me, says the Lord, for I will forgive their evildoing and remember their sin no more."

### Reflection:

Each of us is familiar with contracts. They are issued for insurance policies, for employment, for purchases, for construction, and in this present age, for security and protection in many other areas. Much care is taken to read between the lines, to know well the terms to which we agree. An agreement means approval and holds the party to legal responsibility. An agreement of this sort indicates clearly the absence of a trust level on which parent and child, husband

and wife, brother and sister behave when the service they render is prompted by love.

Though we have not drawn up a carefully worded contract, we are committed to each other and to the members of our parish family by virtue of our baptism. Our membership (on this staff, parish council, society, committee) gives us certain rights and responsibilities. We are here to serve as brothers and sisters in an atmosphere of trust and love. How do we know these are the terms of our agreement? We need only to open ourselves to understand the awesome message God has spoken through Jeremiah, "I will place my law within you and write it upon your heart; I will be your God, and you shall be my people." This is the covenant, the agreement God has with us. He announces that he is our God and he calls us to be his people. Listen to the provisions of the contract — we simply have to accept God's love and forgiveness and we will know him as he is. Is this not a call to image God's love and forgiveness as we work together in serving the needs of our parish?

## Sharing:

(Having provided sufficient time for personal reflection, the leader now calls for response as individuals feel moved to share.)

- What does it mean to be baptized into the Body of Christ?
- How do we live out our baptismal call each day?
- What are some responsibilities which we have to the people of this parish, to the people with whom we work, and to ourselves?
- How can we (as a staff, a parish council, a society, a committee) image God's forgiveness in a particular situation in our parish?

## Prayer:

(All) God, our Father, we praise and thank you for the privilege of being called your people. We often forget, and at times ignore the fact that you as God dwell within us. We often forget, and at times ignore the fact that you have carved your law of love on our hearts. It is this love which you give us — not for ourselves — but to be shared with others. Free us, Father, from the rigidity of legal contracts in our interactions. Show us how to relate as brothers and sisters thus developing a family atmosphere here in                    Parish. We ask this through Jesus, your Son and our brother, whose living among your people provides a model of community for us.

## Suggested Song:

*Earthen Vessels,* John Foley, S.J.

We hold a treasure, not made of gold,
In earthen vessels, wealth untold,
One treasure only: the Lord, the Christ,
In earthen vessels.

1. Light has shown in our darkness:
God has shown in our heart,
With the light of the glory
Of Jesus, the Lord.

2. He has chosen the lowly,
Who are small in this world;
In His weakness is glory,
In Jesus, the Lord.

# A New Creation...
## A People That Walks in Justice

### Call to Prayer:
(The leader calls the members of the community to quiet time apart from the busyness of the day. S/he prays spontaneously or invites one from the group to offer the opening prayer. An invitation of this nature should be extended prior to the gathering time.)

### Scripture:
(The leader or another reverently proclaims the Scripture passage from a Bible, then provides a short time of silence during which the Word of God can infiltrate each person's heart and mind.)

### Isaiah 11:3b-9
"...there shall be no harm or ruin on all my holy mountain."

### Reflection:
(The leader opts to read the reflection aloud or invites one of the group to participate, always allowing preparation time before the session. The leader could suggest that the other members set their books aside during this reading.)

The images which Isaiah's prophecy sketches in our mind are far from the true picture of reality — especially for anyone who has stood at the barred cage of a wolf or a lion — or who may sit in the security of the family room and view the tragic stories of the evening news. What then could be the prediction of these words? As we examine the details of the Scripture passage we are aware that settings such as those described will be common in a world that receives the Lord. The wolves and lions and cobras will no longer be a threat in the forests, and the media will report stories of love.

How will this change come about? How other is Christ the Instrument of Justice in this age, except through his people? Isaiah's prophecy is being unravelled in our midst through God's power at work in each of us.

Let us say with conviction the words of Isaiah with the simple substitution of a pronoun:

Not by appearance shall *we* judge,
nor by hearsay shall *we* decide.
But *we* shall judge the poor with justice
and decide aright for the land's afflicted...
Justice shall be the band around *our* waist
and faithfulness a belt upon *our* hips.
Then class distinctions, racial barriers, superiority/
inferiority, rich/poor, educated/illiterate, young/old, all
divisions will cease and "the earth shall be filled with
knowledge of the Lord."

## Suggested Song:

*A Time Will Come for Singing,* Dan Schutte, S.J.

1. A time will come for singing when all your tears are shed,
   When sorrow's chains are broken, and broken hearts
   shall mend.
   The deaf will hear your singing when silent tongues
   are freed.
   The lame will join your dancing when blind eyes learn
   to see.

2. A time will come for singing when trees will raise
   their boughs,
   When all lay down their armor, and hammer their swords
   into plows,
   When beggars live as princes and orphans find their homes,
   When prison cells are emptied and hatred has grown old.

3. A time will come for singing a hymn by hearts foretold,
   that kings have sought for ages, and treasured more
   than gold.
   Its lyrics turn to silver when sung in harmony.
   The Lord of Love will teach us to sing its melody.

Record Album/Cassette *Gentle Night*
© 1977 North American Liturgy Resources
2110 W. Peoria Avenue, Phoenix, AZ 85029

## Sharing:

(The leader provides sufficient time for individuals to
silently reflect on the questions, then invites the people to
share their insights.)

- How are we making the Lord known within the membership
  (of this staff, council, society, committee)?
- What are some ways in which we can act justly in serving
  the poor, the homeless, the unemployed, the imprisoned,

whose needs have been made known through our social concerns committee, the media, or other persons?

- What can we as a group do this week (or before the next meeting) to bring about change in an unjust situation?

## Petitions:
(The leader invites spontaneous prayers of intercession.)

## Prayer:
(The leader calls the group to pray this closing prayer in unison.)

Lord God, in this moment you reveal yourself to us as a just and faithful God. Since our call is to image you, stir up the power of your Spirit within each one's heart so that we will cast aside any prejudices, conscious or unconscious, with which we have approached this meeting. Dispel from our memories any hearsay which may have fallen on our ears so we may have freed minds in discussing the items on the agenda. Through this openness, Lord, we believe that you will use us as your model in serving your people here in _____ Parish and we together will make your Name known. We ask this in the Name of Jesus, your Son and our brother. Amen.

# A Harvester...
## One Who Plants
## the Word of God

## Call to Prayer:

(The leader prepares for this time of prayer by calling the members into a quiet, restful atmosphere. S/he gently reminds the people to place all distractions before the Lord.)

Lord God, it is good for us to be here. We praise you for your presence in our lives. We thank you for this time of quiet.

## Suggested Song:

*Come With Me Into the Fields,* Dan Schutte, S.J.

1. The fields are high and summer's days are few;
Green fields have turned to gold.
The time is here for the harvesting,
For gathering home into barns.

*Refrain*
The harvest is plenty; laborers are few.
Come with Me into the fields.
Your arms may grow weary; your shoes will wear thin.
Come with Me into the fields.

2. The seeds were sown by other hands than yours;
Nurtured and cared for they grew.
But those who have sown will not harvest them;
The reaping will not be their care.

Record Album/Cassette *Neither Silver Nor Gold*
© 1971 by Daniel L. Schutte, S.J., North American Liturgy Resources, Phoenix, AZ 85029

## Scripture:

(Reading from the Bible, the leader reverently proclaims the Scripture passage. S/he provides a few moments of silence and invites the members of the group to silently read the reflection and questions.)

## Matthew 9:35-38

"...the harvest is good but laborers are scarce. Beg the harvest master to send out laborers to gather his harvest."

## Reflection:

This passage has often been cited as the call of the Christian to pray for vocations to the vowed life and the priesthood. Certainly this response to the Scripture got many a Christian "off the hook."

When the initial call was directed to the Twelve, Jesus was opening up his own mission and power to admit his followers. Today, we his followers, hear the call to proclaim Jesus' peace, love, joy, mercy, compassion, justice, kindness to his people.

Indeed the harvest is ready — the harvest of our parish community, the harvest of our PTA, our youth group, our homebound, our handicapped, our widowed, ourselves. We are the laborers whom the Lord empowers to share in his mission to gather the harvest. As we open our lives to serve others, we discover that they in turn are ministering to us.

## Sharing:

(Having provided sufficient time for personal reflection, the leader now calls for response as individuals feel moved.)

- What do you think is a great need of our parish community, parish council, society, committee?
- Share an experience from your life when the person to whom you ministered was special gift to you.
- What can we do before our next meeting in response to the Lord's call to be laborers of the harvest?

## Petitions:

Include persons whose image passed through your mind as you reflected on the questions.

## Prayer:

(All) Lord Jesus, we hear with newness this call to be a laborer in your vineyard. We acknowledge that this invitation is directed to each of us as a unique person, but we realize that you intend it for us collectively, also. It is your gift of understanding that permits us to make this observation. Now, Lord, we ask you to release the power of your Spirit in our lives so we can identify the areas within our community which at this time need our attention. Show us, Lord, your way to touch the lives of these people. We ask this in your name. Amen.

# A Model for Dialogue...
## Jesus Who Is Word

### Call to Prayer:
(Meditative music played softly creates an atmosphere in which a person can travel within to touch the God who dwells there. The leader selects an appropriate instrumental recording.)

### Opening Prayer:
You are our God! We praise you.
You are our peace! We glorify you.
You are our life! We give you thanks.

### Scripture:
(A member of the group reverently proclaims the Scripture passage from the Bible, then provides silence during which time each one invites the Word to penetrate his/her entire being.)

### Jeremiah 20:9
"I will speak in his name no more. But then it becomes like fire burning in my heart, imprisoned in my bones; I grow weary holding it in!"

### Reflection:
(The leader suggests that the group read the reflection silently, being attentive to the way in which God will reveal his message.)

Jeremiah felt that the situation would have been under control had he been able to do his own thing; but, he followed the direction of the Lord and found himself under persecution. In his mission among the people he would have liked to be popular, to do the building and the planting; however, God was using him to utter some harsh messages. Though Jeremiah tried to suppress his preaching, the power of the Word exploded within.

How often discouragement shackles us to the earth! We decide to move in our own way and fail; we are called upon to risk popularity by confronting a situation; or we prefer to remain uninvolved when leadership is needed. At times we

26

may stubbornly announce that, "We'll just not say another word." Then the Lord reveals his power through an event, a person, a hardship, a plant, a leaf, a teardrop, and we must share this moment of conversion.

## Sharing:

(Having provided private reflection time, the leader calls the members to share responses.)

• How has a smile or an expression of concern or a word of encouragement been such a moment of conversion in your life recently? or not so recently? or even in the distant past?
• How is the Lord calling us to become those moments for our sisters and brothers?
• Describe a situation in which the Lord might ask us to speak in his Name.

## Prayer:

(All) Lord, what a waste of energy trying to hold in your power which is alive within this group! Release our wills, sever the cords which bind our tongues; so that the fire of your words may reach out to singe, scorch, and finally consume all whom we serve. We ask this in Jesus' Name. Amen.

# A Voice for God...
## A Person Who Listens

### Call to Prayer:
(The leader gently calls the membership into a quiet, restful atmosphere.)

God, our Father, we stand in awe as we acknowledge your presence within and among us. Fill us with your gentleness.

### Scripture:
(Using the Bible, the leader reverently proclaims the single verse which is indicated below and provides a few moments of silence so the Word of God can penetrate to the core of each one's heart.)

### Jeremiah 15:19b
"If you bring forth the precious without the vile, you shall be my mouthpiece."

### Reflection:
(Having prepared beforehand, one of the group now reads the reflection. The leader could suggest that the other members set their books aside to listen.)

God as gift-giver calls us to discipleship, to live and to speak as a reflection of himself. He graciously accepts our response regardless of our limitation. He is willing to smooth down the rough spots, to knead out the lumps, to use us as his instruments. At times we make glaring blunders, at times we get tongue-twisted, at times we pull back through fear, and still he speaks through us.

According to his dealings with the prophet Jeremiah, however, we know that there are necessary conditions. God told the prophet, "If you bring forth the precious" — if you eliminate the vile — if, in fact, Jeremiah was willing to have a conversion of his speech pattern, to speak with gentleness and sensitivity towards others, then — and only then — would he be the Lord's mouthpiece.

### Sharing:
(The leader invites the members to silently read all the questions, providing sufficient time for personal reflection. The leader encourages the sharing of responses, allowing

individuals to choose any question with which they feel at ease.)

- Recall a situation in which you were praised. How did you feel? What did you do with the words of praise?
- How do you handle a false accusation? or when blame is implied in another's comment?
- How do you feel when approached with a gentle tone?
- How might you respond to others' limitations, short-comings? — Yes, even during this session?
- What can you do when a 'hot tip' about a person is brought into conversation?

## Prayer:

(All) Lord God, pour out your power to eliminate the prejudiced hearts and minds with which we may have come to this session. Open our senses to see and hear, to touch and feel your life reflected in each other.

Teach us how to separate the precious from the vile —
Teach us how to praise rather than blame —
Teach us how to compliment rather than accuse —
Teach us how to (pause and invite spontaneous additions)

We ask for these conversions through your Son, Jesus.

## Suggested Song:
*Sing Of Him*

Sing of Him softly; sing of Him loud.
Sing His melody ev'rywhere.
Tell of Him slowly; tell as you run.
Tell it to ev'ryone soon.

1. Who could know the wonder of God?
Gaze on His face?
Pronounce His name?
Who could dare to dream to ask
What He has dared to reveal?

2. Ponder it deeply; make it your own.
Welcome Him in to your memory,
gratefully.

Carry it careful; treasure it well;
give it to anyone at all.

3. (instrumental)

4. Dream it at morning; proclaim it at noon.
Whisper it gently at evening,
faithfully.
Tell of Him slowly; tell as you run.
Tell it to ev'ryone soon.

# The Art of Listening...
## A Third Ear That Hears

## Call to Prayer:
(The leader calls the people to prayer by providing a quiet, gentle atmosphere for a few moments.)

## Opening Prayer:
(The leader prays spontaneously or uses the following prayer.)

God, our Father, we praise you for the gentleness of this moment. Absorb our distractions so we might be attentive to your Word.

## Suggested Song:
*Dwelling Place*

1. I fall on my knees to the Father of Jesus,
The Lord who has shown us
The glory of God.

2. May He in His love give us strength for our living,
The strength of His spirit,
The glory of God.

All: May Christ find a dwelling place
of faith in our hearts.
May our lives be rooted in love,
rooted in love.

3. May grace and peace be yours
In God, our Father,
And in His Son.

4. I fall on my knees to the Father of Jesus,
The Lord who has shown us
The glory of God.

Record Album/Cassette — *Dwelling Place*
© 1976 John B. Foley, S.J., North American Liturgy Resources, Phoenix, AZ 85029

## Scripture:

(The leader reverently proclaims the verse from the Bible, providing a short time of silence for the Word to speak to each one's heart.)

## Romans 15:4

"Everything written before our time was written for our instruction, that we might derive hope from the lessons of patience."

## Reflection:

(The leader invites the members of the community to read the reflection silently at a slow, meditative pace, suggesting that they move on to personally reflect on the words provided.)

We wait in the wee hours of the morning for the sunrise and later in the day gaze toward the west in anticipation of the sunset. We are certain — as certain as can be our prediction of the future — that the cycle of the *movement of the sun* will daily repeat itself. How strange that we should catch ourselves re-reading that phrase — the movement of the sun!

How is it that through the years we have been caught in the misconception of sunrise/sunset and have buried the truth that it is the earth which is in constant motion! Do we take time to think about the rotation of the earth as causing the appearance of the arrival and departure of the sun? Does our acceptance of the sunrise/sunset concept raise other questions? Do we believe labels easily and sometimes permit word meanings to create distances in human relationships? Do we take time at our meetings to surface all that a word denotes and connotes? A dictionary can provide a clear definition of a word but only persons can share all the ideas suggested by that term.

## Sharing:

(Having allowed sufficient time for a meditative reading of the reflection and the suggested vocabulary, the leader invites individuals to respond.)

Choose one of the following words: vacation, parent, family, employer. Define the word and then share the ideas which the word suggests (e.g., *dwelling* could be defined as a shelter, a residence, a home, but this word connotes various ideas — security for a child, peace and love for family members, fear

33

for a prodigal child, anxiety for a lonely person, drudgery for a broken person).

Now choose a word which you find in the vocabulary of your committee — church, community, ministry, service, shared responsibility, and share the definition and connotation of the term.

## Prayer:

(All) Lord, reveal to each of us the times when we hold tenaciously to our understanding of a concept and fail to see another's point of view. Open to us new ways of communicating — teach us how to affirm with a smile or a nod, teach us how to console with a gentle touch, teach us how to be honest with ourselves and others, and yes, how to confront with a soft tone. Teach us how to be sensitive to levels of meaning, and how to listen to others' feelings. Teach us how to use the ideas which come from within each member (of this committee, society, staff, parish council). We ask all this in the name of your Son, Jesus. Amen.

# An Aerial View...
## The Look That Calms

### Call to Prayer:

(Arrange a sufficient number of chairs in a circle in one section of the meeting room and have an instrumental piece playing softly. This setting will help to create a prayerful atmosphere into which people can come.)

### Opening Prayer:

(After a few moments of silence, the leader prays.)

Lord God, you are the gentleness and the peace which surrounds us. Touch us in the areas of our lives which are restless in this moment. Free us from all fears and anxieties.

### Scripture:

(The leader or a volunteer approached earlier proclaims the Scripture passage from the Bible.)

### Mark 4:35-41

"...he rebuked the wind and said to the sea: 'Quiet! Be Still!' "

### Suggested Song:

*Be Not Afraid,* Bob Dufford, S.J.

1. You shall cross the barren desert,
But you shall not die of thirst.
You shall wander far in safety
Though you do not know the way.
You shall speak your words in foreign lands
And all will understand.
You shall see the face of God and live.

*Refrain*
Be not afraid.
I go before you always.
Come follow Me,
And I will give you rest.

2. If you pass through raging waters in the sea
You shall not drown.
If you walk amid the burning flames,

You shall not be harmed.
If you stand before the pow'r of hell
And death is at your side,
Know that I am with you through it all.

3. Blessed are your poor,
For the kingdom shall be theirs.
Blest are you that weep and mourn,
For one day you shall laugh.
And if the wicked ones insult and hate you
All because of Me,
Blessed, blessed are you!

## Reflection:

(The leader invites the membership to read the reflection silently at a slow, meditative pace, suggesting that they move on to personally reflect on the questions.)

The ebb and flow of our individual lives reveal a mere glimpse into the movement of persons interacting within groups. No one is singularly protected from storms, from hardships, from rumblings. We are all subject to being tossed by disappointments, being thrown off course by disturbances. At times we would believe and lead others to accept the fact that Jesus has fallen asleep. In some instances we feel that he has forgotten us, or at least he is glancing in an opposite direction! We disregard an encouraging word from a friend or a nudge to look at the situation from another perspective.

It might help, though, to recall a past experience — a time when we were the rescuer for a child caught in the maze of a department store aisle. Our immediate response was to tell the little one to stop crying because everything would be under control. To the youngster, the three-foot cases were skyscrapers and the absence of a familiar face was frightening. The child could not plot out an escape route; however, the adult had clearer vision and could offer a message of hope. When the child was lifted above the obstacles, joy returned — Mommy or Daddy was in sight.

At times we need an aerial view — to have someone lift us above the barriers — to see clearly a new way out.

## Sharing:

(Having provided sufficient time for a meditative reading of the reflection and silent response to the questions, the leader calls for verbal input.)

- What do I sense is an obstacle which could deter us from our assigned task this evening?
- How can I be helpful in lifting us above the barrier of stubbornness, jealousy, self-interest?
- By taking an aerial view of the task at hand, what can I suggest as an alternate plan of action?

## Litany:

(The leader invites the people to pray the litany together, adding personal phrases.)

In times of pain, give us your strength, Lord.

In moments of weakness, give us your strength, Lord.

When we are faced with discouragement, give us your strength, Lord.

When we are thrown off course by disturbances, give us your strength, Lord.

For the sick of our parish, give them your strength, Lord.

(Spontaneous Phrases)

## Prayer:

(All) Father, you are here within us and among us. At times we fail to acknowledge the power which your presence releases in our lives. We depend upon our strength and are easily shaken by the rumblings of the storm. We panic and cry out to you implying that you have abandoned us. In response you calm and console us, not through extraordinary means, but by stirring up an image in our memory. You lead us to the process of recall so we can gently replay an event in our lives in which you were our protector, our guide, our peace. Open us now to be your instruments in calling each other beyond any obstacles as we work for the building of your kingdom here in _____ Parish.

## Prayer to release the pinch of pressure:

(Someone from the group may suggest the use of this prayer in tense moments which arise from unpleasant disagreements, hostility, cutting remarks.)

Lord God, we take a few minutes away from our task of this evening. Stir up within each of us your Spirit of peace and love. We praise and thank you for reminding us that you calm the storms which rage within and among us. You are a gentle God who loves each of us in the depths of our weakness. Strengthen us, Lord, so we will image your patience. We ask this in Jesus' name.

# A Gentle Touch...
## The Glue That Repairs

### Call to Prayer:

(The leader calls the people to be attentive to God's presence within and among them, encouraging them to allow the words of the song to enter their hearts.)

### Suggested Song:

*Lay Your Hands,* Rev. Carey Landry

**Refrain**
Lay Your hands gently upon us.
Let their touch render Your peace.
Let them bring Your forgiveness and healing.
Lay Your hands gently, lay Your hands.

1. You were sent to free the broken hearted.
You were sent to give sight to the blind.
You desire to heal all our illnesses.
Lay Your hands gently, lay Your hands.

2. Lord, we come to You through one another.
Lord, we come to You in our need.
Lord, we come to You seeking wholeness.
Lay Your hands gently, lay Your hands. (Refrain)

Record Album/Cassette *Abba, Father*
ⓒ 1977 North American Liturgy Resources,
2110 W. Peoria Avenue, Phoenix, AZ 85029

### Scripture:

(Prior to the gathering the leader asks three persons to prepare the parts of the reading — narrator, Jesus, Jairus' friend. Using separate Bibles the readers proclaim the Scripture story.)

### Luke 8:40-42, 49-56

"He took her by the hand...the breath of life returned..."

### Reflection:

(The leader invites the group to read the reflection and questions silently at a slow, meditative pace.)

**38**

Enter into the lives of the broken family of Jairus. Be sensitive to the situation that was presented to Jesus. Jairus and his wife were hurting; their only child, a preteen daughter was dying. Though Jesus set out immediately, he was delayed by the demands of the crowds. Can you relate to the anxiety which swelled within Jairus? Can you touch the pain which pierced Jairus when he received the news of his daughter's death? What a void he must have experienced in not being present with his wife to share that moment of grief! Imagine yourself in Jairus' home awaiting his return. Can you sense the hysteria of the mother and the heavy atmosphere created by the mourners? What must they feel when Jesus claims that the child is sleeping? Evidence revealed the truth; all signs of life had disappeared.

Beyond human expectations, the power of Jesus was released through a gentle touch and a simple beckoning, and life was restored to a body which life had vacated. Now, rejoice with the family as they celebrate new life among them!

## Sharing:

(Following a time of silence the leader calls for response as individuals feel moved.)

- What are some areas of brokenness that families are experiencing today?
- Share your observation of a healing of brokenness which has taken place within the group.
- How can we be the gentle touch and the simple beckoning to call new life forth?

## Petitions:

(Individuals offer prayers of intercession.)
Response to petitions: Lord, hear us.

## Prayer:

(All) Jesus, your power is at work in us now. We acknowledge this power and claim it as a source of healing within our parish. There are areas in our committee work, there are voids in our lives, there are broken people in our midst, there are bodies from which life seems to have vacated that need your gentle touch and simple beckoning. Use us, Jesus, as your instruments so together we can rejoice with the family of _____ Parish as we celebrate new life among us!

# "SMALL GROUP SHARING"
# MATERIALS

**The Experience of Lent with the Risen Christ**
*by Sister Catherine Nerney, S.S.J.*
This six-week reflection series invites us to repent and believe the Good News.

**Share Your Bread**
*by Sister Joan Jungerman, S.S.N.D.*
A prayerful, reflective seven-part Lenten booklet designed to help us take stock, and to look for areas in which we must change.

**Building Christian Community**
*by Catherine Martin*
This program is designed for use by all who are willing to make serious efforts to build a Christian community in which loving persons pray and reflect, learn and serve together.

**Spiritual Growth**
*by Sister Joan Jungerman, S.S.N.D.*
This twelve-session booklet, based on St. John's Gospel, calls participants to reflection, prayer, discussion and outreach.

# "SMALL GROUP SHARING"
# RESOURCE BOOKS

**Prayers for the Seasons**
*by Lois Kikkert, O.P.*
A book of prayer experiences designed for use within the entire parish. Its purpose is to provide a prayerful atmosphere from which any business meeting can flow.

**Building for Justice: A Guide for Social Conerns Committees**
*ed. John Bins*
A guidebook filled with practical helps and suggestions for parish social concerns groups as they start and as they grow.

**Moving Toward Small Christian Communities, An On-Going Model of Parish Life**
*by Msgr. Thomas A. Kleissler, Catherine Martin, and Rev. Joseph T. Slinger*
A booklet designed to show how small communities can be an integral part of parish life.

**Thy Kingdom Come**
*by Mary Elizabeth Clark, S.S.J.*
A collection of twenty-four prayer sessions designed to provide a spiritual foundation for social concerns groups.

# "SMALL GROUP SHARING"
# PRAYER LEAFLETS
## (for your parishioners during Lent)

**Change and Believe!**
*by Rev. Kenneth J. St. Amand*
A collection of thoughts for each day of Lent for those Christians interested in responding to the invitations of Christ during this season of grace.

**Journey With Paul**
*by Rev. John J. Gilchrist*
Brief Scriptual reflections and comments contained in a pocket-size booklet of daily Lenten meditations.

55